Chickens

Camilla de la Bédoyère

QED Publishing

Editor: Eve Marleau
Designer: Melissa Alaverdy
Picture Researcher:
      Maria Joannou

Copyright © QED Publishing 2010

First published in the UK in 2010 by
QED Publishing
A Quarto Group company
226 City Road
London EC1V 2TT

www.qed-publishing.co.uk

A catalogue record for this book is available
from the British Library.

ISBN 978 1 84835 448 7

Printed and bound in China

Words in **bold**
are explained in
the Glossary on
page 22.

Picture credits
(t=top, b=bottom, l=left, r=right, c=centre,
fc=front cover)

Alamy Images Inga Spence 20tr; Corbis Louis
Laurent Grandadam 8-9, Justin Guariglia 10l;
Getty Images The Image Bank/Bob Elsdale 4, 5bl,
Photographer's Choice/Georgette Douwma 5t, First
Light/Bert Klassen 6-7, Jean Michel Foujols 7t, AFP/
Frederick Florin 12t, Dorling Kindersley/Kim Taylor
and Jane Burton 14t, Taxi/VCL 14b, Dorling
Kindersley/Peter Anderson 17t; **Photolibrary** Jeff
Friedman 9t, Lasting Images 11b, Alberto Paredes
12-13, Oxford Scientific Film/Roger de la Harpe 13t,
Juniors Bildarchiv 18-19b; **Shutterstock** Vasyl
Helevachuk cc, Lilya cl, cr, Eric Isselée 2t, 21t, Iakov
Kalinin 2-3, 14-15, Oleg Kirillov 2-3b, MisterElements
3t, 5br, 7b, 10r, 12b, 15bl, 17b, 18b, 20br, Hydromet 4-5,
Arnaud Weisser 6l, Fat_fa_tin 6r, Ivaylo Ivanov 11t,
Tischenko Irina 15t, Lilya 15br, 20l, Smit 16-17, Thumb
18-19t, Monkey Business Images 19r, S.Cooper Digital
21b, Vasyl Helevachuk 22, Yuliyan Velchev 22-23,
Michael Woodruff 24.

Contents

What are chickens?

Chickens are birds. Like all birds, chickens have feathers and beaks, and they lay eggs.

Chickens have wings, but they are not very good at flying. Farmers clip some of their wing feathers, to stop chickens flying away from the farm.

⬇ Male chickens are usually larger than females. They can be brightly coloured.

wing

foot

comb

A chicken's mouth is called a beak.

There is a piece of flesh on top of a chicken's head that looks like a crown. It is called a comb.

beak

head

wattle

⬆ Another piece of flesh hangs below the chicken's beak. This is called a wattle.

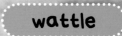

Farmyard Fact!

Combs and wattles help chickens to keep cool. The male chicken's bright-red wattle helps him to attract females.

Chickens on the Farm

Chickens are kept on farms all over the world. There are hundreds of different breeds, or types, of chicken.

Chickens are large birds. They measure about 30 to 40 centimetres from their feet to the top of their head. That's about as tall as a large box of cereal.

FRUITY CEREAL

625g

⇦ Chickens can fluff out their feathers, which makes them look even bigger.

Chickens lived in the wild until people began keeping chickens for food. Now, there are more chickens in the world than people. Most chickens are kept for their meat or eggs.

⇦ Hens can be very friendly, and like to be stroked.

⇧ The large chicken is a cockerel. The other chickens are hens.

Farmyard Fact!

Male chickens are called roosters or cockerels, and females are called hens. Baby chickens are called chicks.

Where do chickens live?

Most chickens live on poultry farms. A poultry farmer keeps only birds such as chickens and turkeys.

Chickens spend the night in barns. The floors of barns are covered in straw, and there are **perches** for the chickens to sleep on.

During the day, the chickens wander around the farmyard in the fresh air.

⇩ When the sun is shining, the hens go outside. If it rains, they can go back into their barn.

⇩ Hens grip onto their perches with their strong, clawed feet.

Farmyard Fact!

Chickens often sleep with one eye open, or they tuck their head under one of their wings.

What do chickens eat?

Chickens do not have any teeth, so they have to eat small pieces of food. They swallow this food whole.

Farmers put out water and feeders for their chickens. Feeders are full of chicken feed, which is made of grains such as wheat and barley.

⇧ Chickens spend a lot of time eating. They peck at their food.

Farmyard Fact!

Farmers give hens bits of broken seashells, called grit, to eat. Grit helps hens to lay eggs with strong shells.

← Grains of wheat are small and full of goodness.

When chickens go outside, they scratch the ground with their claws. They look for worms, insects and small seeds to eat.

Sometimes, chickens ⇨ eat grass.

The life cycle of chickens

Hens start to lay eggs when they are about five months old. They can lay up to 300 eggs in one year.

Eggs will not grow into chicks unless a rooster has **mated** with the hen, and **fertilized** her eggs.

2

Hens lay their eggs in nests. They sit on the eggs to keep them warm.

1

About three weeks later, the chicks are ready to **hatch** out.

3

⬆ Once the chicks' feathers have dried, they become fluffy.

The chicks grow into ⬜➡ adults in a few months, and the life cycle begins again.

4

Farmyard Fact!

The **yolk** inside an egg would have been food for a chick, if the egg had been fertilized.

Why do we farm chickens?

Poultry farmers collect the fertilized eggs. They keep them in a place called a hatchery.

Hatcheries are warm places where eggs can hatch into chicks. A few days after they have hatched, the chicks are sorted into two groups.

⬆ Eggs are kept warm so the chicks inside them can grow.

Farmyard Fact!

As hens get older they lay fewer eggs, but their eggs get bigger. When the weather is cold, hens may stop laying eggs altogether.

Some chicks will become **layers**. These chickens will lay eggs to be eaten, or eggs that will become chicks. Some chicks will become **broiler** chickens. Broilers are birds that are grown for their meat.

⇧ Chicks peck at food in the red **feeders**.

⇦ This chick is still hatching from its egg.

Daily life on the farm

Chickens live in groups called flocks. Every few weeks, farm inspectors check that the chickens are being kept well and are healthy.

Some poultry farmers let their chickens roam outside. They are called free-range chickens, and they lay free-range eggs.

⇩ Little chicks stay near the hens, where they feel safe.

Free-range chickens are able to walk around and look for food. At night, they return to their barns, or to small houses called coops, to sleep.

Farmyard Fact!

Chickens love dust and dirt. They ruffle their feathers in the dirt to help to keep their feathers clean and in good condition.

⬆ Chickens like to explore the ground near their coop. Sometimes they escape!

From the farm to the table

Farmers keep hens so they can sell their eggs. Some farmers sell their chickens as food.

Eggs are put into egg boxes. The eggs are sent to shops and supermarkets. Eggs can also be used to make other foods, such as cakes and biscuits.

Egg boxes hold eggs ⇧ in place, so they do not move around and break.

These hens are layers. They ⇨ will each lay about five eggs a week.

Farmyard fact!

When eggs are cooked, the heat changes the runny insides of an egg into a solid.

When broiler chickens are more than 20 weeks old, they are taken to a slaughterhouse. Their meat is packed and sold fresh or frozen in shops and supermarkets.

Chicken meat is full of goodness ⇨ to help you stay healthy.

Breeds

Chickens come in all shapes, sizes and colours. The different kinds of chicken are called breeds.

Leghorns have white feathers and are mostly kept on farms for their eggs. Most breeds of chicken lay white, cream or brown eggs, but some lay blue or dark-brown eggs.

⇧ Farmers get paid more for large eggs, or for ones with different colours.

leghorn chicken

⇧ Leghorn hens are fast movers, and can fly over fences.

Farmyard Fact!

Buff Orpington chickens are very popular. They are a light-gold colour and lay large brown eggs.

Polish crested chicken

Some breeds are kept for their looks. Chickens with crests, strong colours and pretty feathers are popular.

Bantams are small chickens. They are often very colourful and can be kept as pets.

⇧ Polish crested chickens have fluffy feathers on their heads, called crests.

bantam chicken

⇧ Bantam hens lay very small eggs.

21

Glossary

Broiler
A broiler chicken is one that is kept for its meat.

Feeder
Food containers for chickens are called feeders.

Fertilize
When a special cell from a male joins a female's egg to form a new living thing.

Hatch
This is when a chick breaks out of its egg.

Inspector
A person who checks that animals on farms are looked after well is called an inspector.

Layer
A hen that is kept for her eggs is called a layer.

Mate
When a cockerel and hen come together to fertilize the hen's eggs they are said to mate.

Perch
The place where hens like to stand or sit is called a perch.

Poultry
Birds that are kept on farms are called poultry. The word 'poultry' is also used for the meat that comes from those birds.

Yolk
The yellow part of an egg is called the yolk.

Index

Notes for parents and teachers

Talk about the basic needs that animals and humans share, such as food, space and shelter. Encourage the child to think about how wild animals get their food and find shelter.

It is fun to find ways that animals are similar, or different to one another – and observing these things is a core science skill. Children could draw pictures of animals with four legs, or ones that eat plants, for example, and go on to identify those that are both plant-eaters and four-legged.

Be prepared for questions about how animals become the meat that we eat. It helps children understand this part of the food chain if they can see it in context: all animals live and die, and farm animals are bred for this purpose.

Cooking together is a great opportunity to have fun and learn. Following a recipe allows a child to practise their reading and measuring skills, follow instructions, chat and be creative. Point out the ways that food changes as ingredients are mixed, heated or cooled. Talk about eating a balanced diet, and the benefits we receive from the different food groups, including meat, milk and eggs.